There's Strength in Your Wings

There's Strength in Your Wings

Experiencing Your Life Through the Metamorphosis of the Butterfly

Jessica Anderson

XULON PRESS

Xulon Press
2301 Lucien Way #415
Maitland, FL 32751
407.339.4217
www.xulonpress.com

Scripture quotations taken from the King James Version (KJV) – *public domain*.

Maya Angelou. (2013, May 15)
    We delight in the beauty of the butterfly, but rarely admit the changes it has gone through to achieve that beauty.
    https://m.facebook.com/story.php?story_fbid=1015182967579796&id=33512954795

The Butterfly Life Cycle
    National Geographic Kids
    https://www.natgeokids.com/nz/discover/animals/insects/butterfly-life-cycle/

Printed in the United States of America.

ISBN-13: 9781545658475

We delight in the beauty of the butterfly, but rarely admit the changes it has gone through to achieve that beauty.

Maya Angelou

Acknowledgements

Thank you to my parents, Jesse J. Anderson and Annette M. Anderson. Thank you both for leading by example. Daddy, thank you for showing me at the age of 9 that you believed I could do anything. Momma, thank you for showing me how important it is to always show gratitude. Thank you both for teaching me the importance of God being the head of my life. Thank you for your unfailing, unconditional love; because of both of you I know agape love, and how to extend it.

To my brothers, Cornelius Green and Thomas Anderson, thank you for your unwavering love, support and encouragement.

To my best friend, Wintra Roby for your very strong opinion, wise counsel and always telling me what I need to hear even when I don't want to hear it.

To my college roommate turned dear friend, Kenyetta Jordan for your open perspective, wise counsel and sound advice.

And to my awesome family, and inner circle of friends who cover me in prayer, and remind me of who and Whose I am which ultimately led me to discover there's strength in my wings; I thank you. I appreciate you and I'm forever grateful for you all.

Contents

Introduction

SPOILER ALERT: You're Gonna Make It!

*J*f you've ever been perplexed about a season of your life this book is for you. Even the most radical believers need reminders from time to time that everything is going to be okay. I pray that you will allow this book to serve as one of those reminders. Though we will be activating our child-like faith throughout this book; there won't be anything childish going on. I'll go ahead and get the disclaimers out the way. I love Jesus. I believe He died on the cross so that we could be saved and have eternal life. I also believe in the yoke destroying power of His word. He doesn't want us burdened and in yoke with the troubles of this world. God wants us to be in yoke with Him. His word says that He will give us rest and that His burden is light. (Matthew 11:28-30) The older I become the more I realize the importance of positive thoughts and having a vision for my life. They both need to be aligned in order to fuel your purpose. You must have a vivid picture in your mind of what you would like to one day see manifest in your life. Just like some people need glasses because their vision is not what it used to be. You must do that mentally to improve the vision for your life.

Habakkuk 2:2-3 stresses the importance of putting your vision and plans on paper.

And the Lord answered me, and said, write the vision, and make it plain upon tables, that he may run that readeth it.

For the vision is yet for an appointed time, but at the end it shall speak, and not lie: though it tarry, wait for it; because it will surely come, it will not tarry.

Of course I wasn't familiar with that verse as a child, but it makes so much sense to me now. You have to mentally see it before you can ever see it in the natural. It's true we can't control what comes to our mind, but we are absolutely responsible for the thoughts we allow to stick around. Clear everything that would dare stand in the way of you seeing your dreams clearly.

Our lives can be changed completely when we shift our thinking and take control of our thoughts. Though I like eagles because they soar high and feast on living things, this read was birthed as a result of me following after my vision, tapping into my child-like faith and my lifelong favorite; the butterfly.

In this book I've used the analogy of the stages taken for the caterpillar to become a butterfly compared to the different seasons we go through in life to express the ease it would be to make transitions if we would only change our perspective.

For as long as I can remember I have been fond of butterflies. There's just something about the bright colored wings and the way they fly around so freely that always makes me happy. Couple that with my enjoyment of reading and writing and that is how this journey began; a very long time ago.

As a child one of the gifts I often received were the Lisa Frank journals and diaries. Of all the gifts I received, those became my favorite. If you're familiar with her stuff at all you know they were bold eye catching colors. I would write everything in those journals and I continue to do the same as an adult. I love beautiful bright colored journals, and now I enjoy ones with motivational quotes or scriptures. Although I didn't know at the time, but writing would become one of my favorite things to do, and is still a favorite pass time of mine as an adult. The bible says that in order to enter into heaven we must become like children. (Matthew 18:3)

I personally believe it says that because of the innocence of the child. Children haven't had a chance to allow pride and arrogance to enter their hearts and they are still teachable. Every other Sunday I mentor the children at my church's Word Kids Ministry, and over the course of these last 5 years one thing that always stands out is their innocence. I mentor to serve them, but the truth is they serve me. I learn so much from them. The faith behind some of the prayers I've heard from my 8 and 9 year olds is unbelievable.

Wherever you are in your life right now I challenge you to tap into that child-like faith. Go back to the first time you learned about the life cycle of the butterfly. You were probably a child, right? Butterflies go through a process called complete metamorphosis, and although humans don't go through metamorphosis there are some things in life that change us forever. We couldn't go back to the way we were before even if we tried.

Throughout this book you'll find 4 subsections that will introduce you to the following chapters. There are 4 because of the stages in the butterfly life cycle. Though completely different species there is insight that can be gained from this analogy. You'll also have an opportunity to check in with self and "do your work", you'll be reminded of how to keep your thoughts and vision in line while in pursuit of your purpose and for times when you only have a few moments, but need a quick reminder of God's love; you'll find nuggets of wisdom.

Life's disappointments and setbacks can easily leave us feeling overwhelmed and discouraged. My prayer is that you would begin to shift your mindset. I want to remind you that even when everything around you looks bleak and uncertain; God is faithful. He will use that thing that you thought broke you to position you.

What's stopping you from spreading your wings? Do you even realize that you have them? Everything you need to succeed is already inside of you. Maybe you've seen so much failure that you begin to expect it now. Or has your heart been broken to the point that you know you will never be the same again? Have you considered that maybe God doesn't want you the same? As crazy as it may sound maybe you're right where God wants you. Broke, hurt, divorced. Will you still praise Him? Do you believe that He will deliver, heal and restore you?

Have you allowed fear to keep you in a place of complacency? Just how bad do you want to come out of that place? Or maybe every time you attempt to make a bold move you're hit with the crippling mistakes and failures of your past? Ask yourself how passionate you are about your goals. Ask yourself how passionate you are about leaving a legacy for your children. Have you begun to feel different, and you wonder if depression may be trying to creep in? Questioning your mental health? Nah, of course not. Mental illness couldn't possibly happen to you? You should know that mental illness does not attach its self to a certain socioeconomic class. Have you cried out for God to take you now, surely death is better than your current state. Thoughts of hurting yourself and suicide are from the pits of hell! Cast those thoughts down, and seek professional help if you need to. Is it addiction? God has given us dominion over everything in the earth, which means nothing that grows from or is created in earth should have power over you.

And God said, Let us make man in our image, after our likeness: and let them have dominion over the fish of the sea, and over the fowl of the air, and over the cattle, and over all the earth, and over every creeping thing that creepeth upon the earth. (Genesis: 1:26)

Whom the son sets free is free indeed. Do you want to be free? Whatever you're dealing with I pray that you will use your child-like faith to gain a new perspective. Gain a fresh outlook on the different seasons of your life, and allow yourself to be completely transformed by the renewing of your mind. (Romans 12:2)

What's that you're feeling? The atmosphere is getting ready to change. God is about to do a miraculous work in you, and I pray you will allow it. Allow the message of this book, and the Holy Spirit to be a guide in helping you understand that everything you need is already inside of you. I pray you get your heart and mind in line with what God says about you and not man. Yes, your heart too. I know many have gotten used to not involving their heart, but your heart has to be included in this journey. Every part of you must be a willing participant. Everything that comes in your life comes through your heart. (Proverbs 4:23) We should ask God to renew our spirit and fix our hearts. (Psalm 51:10)

We do all these fancy cleanses and detox fads, but never think to do a heart cleanse.

They haven't made a concealer yet that'll cover the blemishes on your heart. It matters not how much makeup you put on, how many puppy dog ears or flower headbands or big glossy eye filters you add to your pictures. It doesn't matter how many letters you add behind your name, or if you pledge ABC or XYZ; if you don't get your heart right you won't be any good to yourself or anyone else. There is strength in your wings, and my prayer is that you'll do the work. Seek complete healing for past wounds. Get counseling. Do whatever you need to do in the natural, and trust God to do the Supernatural. Do your work; so that God can do His work through you.

Stage I

"Before I formed you in the womb I knew you, before you were born I set you apart; I appointed you as a prophet to the nations." (Jeremiah 1:5)

Human~Embryo   Butterfly~Egg

Still waiting. Patiently…

*I*f you're waiting on something that means you are in expectation of it. At some point you expect to receive it. Waiting can be a tricky thing. It is so important that we understand that delayed does not automatically mean denied. We must also understand that how we wait is just as important as the waiting. Have you prepared for what you're waiting for? Do your part. Do all you can while you wait patiently on God to fulfill his promises. If anyone understands waiting it's an expecting mother. After the egg and sperm meet the fertilized egg will go on to begin to form human life. Mothers expect that at 40 weeks they will be blessed with a healthy baby. Female butterflies lay their eggs on plants, and those plants become food for the soon to be caterpillars. While waiting many changes will occur with humans and butterflies but the most important thing in this stage is for mom to protect the egg.

I remember the first and only time I became pregnant. Even at 23 there was an instant fear that came because I wasn't married, and I was apprehensive as to how my parents would feel. Those feelings passed quickly as the excitement began to overcome me with the thought of holding my sweet baby. I love children. I must have taken like 5 home tests before I made an appointment to my doctor. The excitement took over me as I made the appointment. I told the receptionist how far along I could have been, and she said, "oh great, you'll be able to hear a heartbeat when you come." I went to my appointment on my lunch break not knowing that I wouldn't be returning to work that day. You see there are some things in life you simply cannot plan for. As I was laying on the table getting an ultrasound there was an uneasiness on the techs face. I knew something wasn't right, but nothing could have prepared me for what came next.

The nurse left the room, and came back to repeat the ultrasound then she went on to say, "I don't hear a heartbeat". "We have to do an emergency surgery." Just like that the very thing I went for I could not receive. I don't care how much of a planner you are there are times when things just won't go as planned. It's in these times that we must understand there is nothing we could have done differently. The enemy usually sends attacks around these times. The enemy is a liar, a master manipulator and is strategic in coming after us when we're already at a low point. That's why it's crucial that we know Gods word so that we can stand on it.

I remember waking up from surgery, and the nurse was explaining everything that went on. She said, because of where your baby lodged the doctor also had to remove your right tube. I say baby intentionally because even at 8 weeks and only being the size of a blueberry I had begun to prepare for what I was going to receive; my baby. We could possibly change the tejectory of our lives if we started operating in the spirit of what we expected to receive. Things like preparing to be a wife or husband before the marriage. Or serving others children before we are blessed with our own. The nurse mentioned a few other things as to how I would feel, and to be honest everything she was saying was a blur because I only wanted to know one thing. Would I still be able to have children? Once she assured me that I would; I was okay. She told me it may be harder to conceive once I got ready, but I would be able to. I just want everyone to know we have to give God something to work with. The nurse telling me it may be harder to conceive wasn't a problem to me. I trust God. Completely. He only needs a willing vessel. God can do anything we allow Him to do in and through our lives. We just have to be sure to give Him the glory. As stated in scripture above, "I set you apart", "I knew you" God is intentional. He knows what He's doing, and if you ever realize you're different; don't fight it. Don't attempt to fit in; you were never supposed to. What's okay for everyone else will never be okay with you. I know waiting can be tedious, and rejection hurts, but trust that it may simply be God's redirection. Dig deeper. Let Him use you and resist the urge to shrink and stay small. Still waiting. Patiently...

My Soul is Anchored

To be anchored means to hold fast or provide a firm hold. Some relate to fishing. Once you have your boat in a place you don't mind being you toss over your anchor with the expectation of it not moving.

It's so important that you are properly anchored. The storms of life can often resemble the winds and waves of the sea, but I want you to know you don't have to wander through life adrift. The storms in your life may be raging, but being anchored to God means you'll be steadfast; unmovable.

Most people don't know but my senior year in high school I was approached by my English teacher to write an essay for a scholarship. I've always enjoyed writing, but thoughts of fear came about that maybe my essay wouldn't be good enough to receive the scholarship. I mean jotting my personal thoughts was cool, but surely my writing wasn't good enough for a scholarship. The topic was about overcoming adversity. I felt like I was capable, but the enemy wanted to plant so many seeds of fear and doubt in my mind that I wouldn't even try. What's inside of you that the enemy wants to keep you from bringing forth? **Don't Fall For It!**

After getting over those feelings and tapping into my love of writing more; I wrote the essay and received the scholarship. Thank God for my teacher seeing something in me, that I hadn't seen in myself. I got to start college without the burden of loans. You wanna know what I do now? I tell everyone I know with graduating seniors about this scholarship, and how they helped me. I'm sure if we are honest with ourselves we would be able to admit to not pursuing a dream or goal because of doubt and fear.

It wasn't until I grew older that I began to gain an understanding of how important it is to be anchored. For me, my faith and belief system along with my love for God is what keeps me grounded. It's what I'm anchored to. Throughout life we will have countless things that will come against what we believe. You have to make a conscious decision to not be moved.

I'm not saying you won't be bothered, just don't be moved. In this social media crazed world the first place people tend to run to when they are "unbothered" is social media. Don't! As soon as you post how "unbothered" you are it lets everyone know that you are just the opposite; bothered. We also showcase how immature we are, and how incapable we are in expressing ourselves and communicating as adults. Sadly, our communication has been cut down to the reposting of memes and misunderstood text messages. Take it to God first. I'm sure once you talk it over with God you will not be lead to air your feelings out on social media. When frustration, doubt, or disappointment creeps in like we know they will; cast those thoughts down. Do NOT allow those thoughts to stick around. My personal favorite is to write down the opposite of what the enemy is attempting to attack me with. Failure, nah, "I can do all things through Christ who strengthens me." (Philippians 4:13)

That didn't go how I wanted it to, nah, Jeremiah 29:11 says God has a plan for my future that will prosper and not harm me. Hold fast to what Gods word says, not man. I don't make a habit of speaking on things I don't know about so if it were not so I wouldn't mention it. Life doesn't care that it's your birthday. Life doesn't care that it's your anniversary. Life doesn't care that you've started a new career path, and need to be trained. Life is not concerned that you have family in town. I know all about the tools the enemy uses by sending thoughts that attack your character, and the very core of who you are. So again, what sustains you? What are you anchored to? Grab a hold to the word of God and its truth and rest in the comfort that God's unfailing love provides.

~Prayer~

God, keep me forever mindful that you're my anchor. God help me to stand on your word. Lord I ask that you would shape me, and mold me to be more like you. Help me to not be moved by adversity or the circumstances around me. God give me the strength to cast down any thoughts that don't line up with your word; anything that doesn't line up with what you've said about me. God help me to maintain a positive mindset. Lord I want to be confident in your word, not puffed up or proud. Lord I seek and follow after your wisdom for I know that you won't lead me astray. In Jesus name, Amen.

Fear is NOT Welcome Here

$\mathcal{W}$e've all heard that fear has killed more dreams than failure ever will. I have to agree. I can honestly attest to allowing fear to kill a few of mine. I can't stress enough how important it is NOT to allow this to happen. The time is going to pass anyway, you may as well pursue your dreams. Everything changed once I began to tap into my God given gift; that we all possess...we just have to access it. Wisdom, knowledge, faith, discerning of spirits...just to name a few. The word of God says the gifts of the spirit are how God enables us to do the work He has called us to do.

2nd Timothy 1:7 says, For the Lord hath not given us the spirit of fear; but of power and of love, and a sound mind. I love that scripture, but in quoting it we must be mindful of the verses that follow which warn us of the afflictions that will surely come. We may be afflicted on every side, but the same God that has called us for His purpose is the same God that has equipped us. He will send us not for our own selfish desires, but for His glory. We must understand that Gods plan may look completely different from our plan, but we must learn to trust Him in spite of that fact. We must be willing to completely surrender ourselves and be transformed for the glory of God. Transformation can be uncomfortable. When you turn everything over to God it will cause everything around you to be different. You'll become cautious of the places you go, and the company you keep. You'll get ready to speak, then pause to be sure your words are edifying. You will begin to command your very thoughts get in line. Most of the battles we face anyway start in our own minds first. Many of us are being held captive by our very own false thoughts. It doesn't matter if these thoughts were brought on by someone else or if you feel them about yourself. Stop it today! You have complete control over what thoughts you allow to hang around. No one is saying you need to be a bible scholar; neither am I one however, it is important that you get yourself a few scriptures that you can speak over your life. Speak them over your situation until you begin to feel a shift in the atmosphere. Speak them until you begin to see what you've said. When fear comes knocking, answer with faith. Be bold, be brave and decree and declare that fear won't have your dreams, fear won't have your family, and fear is not welcome and has no place in any area of your life.

~Prayer~

Lord, I know you haven't given me the spirit of fear. Help me to remember that Faith and fear cannot co-exist. Lord, cause me to remember your word that says I should have a sound mind. Lord, help me to release my own negative thoughts. God set me free from the negative things that have been spoken over my life. Lord be a gatekeeper over my mouth and help me to always speak life and not death; for it is in the very power of my tongue. Help me to not be paralyzed by the fear of the unknown but to walk boldly into the wonderful future that you have for me. In Jesus name, Amen.

Stage II

" But he answered and said, it is written, Man should not live by bread alone but by every word that procedeth out of the mouth of God." Matthew 4:4

Human ~ Infant, Child   Butterfly ~ Caterpillar

All You Can Eat

I don't care for buffets, but that's definitely what stage II is all about. Eating lots of food.

So naturally during this stage parents will be doing everything for their infants. It is the parent's responsibility to make sure they are cleaned, diapers changed and most importantly fed. Food is important for the nourishment of our bodies, but not just any food. Filet Minion may sound appealing, but we wouldn't want to give that to our newborn. We should start them off slow with milk, cereal, and then solid foods. (1 Corinthians 3:2) We have to be sure their systems are able to digest what we give them. It's no different for us as adults, its detrimental to our well-being if we receive something too soon. Always remember timing is everything.

During this stage the caterpillar has one job, and that is to eat all they can. It's important they get as much food as possible as it will be stored and used when they become an adult. It's ironic that they can store up so much food this early and it still be good for later use. It's no different from the different seasons we go through in life. There will be tests, but we must turn those into testimonies. There can't be any victories, if we don't go through the battle. That is why it is so important that we feed ourselves with positivity and study Gods word. Bodily exercise is great, (I Timothy 4:8) but we must also lift that word daily so that we can become mentally strong. You wouldn't get in the ring without boxing gloves so why are you out here trying to win at life without the word of God?

Adversities will arise, and we must be able to bring that knowledge to the front of our minds in order to overcome them. During this stage the caterpillar will significantly grow in size, which is a key point in this stage. Growth. Sadly, many are growing older but not wiser. The most important thing is that we grow through, not just go through.

You Don't Know Me... You Knew Me.

As we are busy declaring Gods word over our lives there will still be attacks, except now we should know how to handle them. I don't believe there is any attack quite like the one our past sends. Being defeated or rejected. Not knowing better, so unable to do better. Knowing better, and still making the wrong decision. Being wronged or thinking that you've been wronged; are all ways that can leave us feeling defeated, but we don't have to accept that.

We all know someone who spends too much energy focusing on their past; or maybe it's you. The truth is though it may be in the past if you're re- living it constantly you're really doing yourself a huge disservice. You're inflicting pain on yourself. Not only are you torturing yourself, but your mistake still controls you. We've all been aggravated by someone who says they forgive us, then turn around and bring the offense up at every given opportunity. Well think about it, that's exactly what you do when you don't forgive yourself. Forgive the people that hurt you, and forgive yourself so that you can move forward with conviction and make better choices. We also make the huge mistake of searching for our future in our past. Why? It does not reside there. We tend to do that very often with relationships. Okay, Timmy didn't head butt you like

Vinny but the relationship is still no good for you. Take all those lessons and start anew.

If we're honest we would all probably do a few things differently. Thank God for hindsight, right? It's definitely 20/20. I wouldn't completely undo those wrong turns; it's from some of those that I've learned the most. When God delivered the Israelites they had been in bondage so long that mentally they were still captive. What are you still in bondage to? Do you not realize that Gods already forgiven you for that? Think about that person you've come across that's living their entire present life based on something that happened 10 years ago. It's just not healthy. Let the past go and let God lead you. He's no longer hanging on to that mistake so why should you?

It's like that old car in the yard with flat tires or the blown engine. Of course it has potential to go simply because it's a car, but if you don't air up the tires and repair the broken engine you won't be going anywhere. Let's say the engine of that car is the heart of your temple. What repairs do you need in order to get moving? What do you need to fix in your heart? What's in your heart that is affecting your vision?

> A good man out of the good treasure of his heart bringeth forth that which is good; and an evil man out of the evil treasure of his heart bringeth forth that which is evil: for of the abundance of the heart his mouth speaketh. (Luke: 6:45)

"For of the abundance of the heart the mouth speaks".

Yes, that's right. If there is an ABUNDANCE of something coming out of your mouth, that means there is an ABUNDANCE of it in your heart. Bitterness, hate, gossip, jealousy; rid yourself of it all. Ask yourself what you need to release from your heart in order to see and speak clearly and get moving with your life. Jesus is the only one who can meet our deepest needs, trust Him and then allow Him to do so. Don't be that car. (Philippians 3:8)

~Prayer~

God, your word says there is a season to everything. Help me to accept when seasons in my life have changed. God give me the wisdom and the strength to keep moving forward and not look back. Lord please make it forever clear to me that my future is not in my past. Lord help me to break strong holds and soul ties that keep me bound to my past. Lord help me to break any patterns that keep me in bondage. In Jesus name, Amen.

Faith On a Million

The word says, the just shall live by faith, and faith comes by hearing the word of God (Romans 1:17) (Romans 10:17)

*O*perating in your faith can be a daily challenge, but I want to help make it easier for you. We learn the words to our favorite songs by listening to them over and over again. It's no different with the word of God, if we want to know what it says we have to study it. If faith comes by hearing that means, we need to pray and ask God to show us what we need to see. Ask God to help us understand as we read. How can you recall what you have not heard? Ask God to reveal himself to you in ways like never before as you read. We also need to be under the leadership of someone teaching the truth about God and His word. I study for myself, but being under the leadership of my Pastor has completely changed my life.

Use caution though because people will attempt to make you feel foolish for having crazy faith. The truth is they may not share it with you but everyone exercises some level of faith. I've heard people say things like, "I have faith the Lord is going to bless me with a new car." Well, okay no harm there but you went in the dealership with a 740 credit score, and you earn a decent living. It didn't require much faith to believe God for that new car. I want you to understand its levels to this faith walk, and I would love to see us take the limits off God and stop making Him so small.

My best friend, Wintra often jokes with me about how my faith is set up. I'll be the first to admit I have the kind of faith that runs the risk of making me look crazy to some people. I don't mind. I take God at His word, and I believe He will do just what He said. Even if the timing doesn't look like I thought it would. I think this is the kind of faith we should all operate in. I wonder how much better our lives would be if we began to have crazy faith. I'm talking radical faith. Nothing tangible, but faith in God to restore our brokenness, and broken relationships. Faith in God to make us whole. Faith in God to perform miracles and heal our bodies of sickness and disease. Faith in God to keep us mentally healthy and in perfect peace. That doesn't mean your faith won't be tested. There are some trials that come, and shine a light on the emptiness in our lives. Those are the very times that you must put your crazy faith into action. Those same unfortunate times are usually breeding ground for growth. Sometimes your faith is all you have. What are you doing to build your faith? If you were stripped of everything else, and left with only your faith would you survive? Would you let fear take over? My prayer is that we would make a decision to choose Faith over fear daily.

~Prayer~

Dear God, I know I'm not perfect, but help me to understand that there's a perfect work being done in and through me. As strong as my faith is there are times when I question my present. Times when I ponder upon what the future holds. God help me to cast my cares on you; for the weight is much too heavy for me to bear. Lord I lay my burdens down at your feet, and I vow not to pick them up again. Lord I trust you. Keep me forever mindful that I'm a warrior and not a worrier. In Jesus name, Amen.

Stage III

"But the God of all grace, who hath called us unto his external glory by Christ Jesus, after that ye have suffered a while, make you perfect, stablish, strengthen, settle you. (1Peter 5:10)

Human ~ Adolescence   Butterfly ~ Chrysalis

#1 Constant is Change

This is the transition stage. We all know about transitions, and how uncomfortable they can make us. As I've stated time and time again I have found that some of the most uncomfortable situations have yielded the most amazing change in my life. I would not tell you if it were not so. Some of that change has felt downright miserable. Miserable I tell you, but there's something about having the peace of God that gets you through the toughest times. Pray, cry, take some slow deep breaths, cry some more, pray some more, get direction, feel the fear, feel the pain, and do it anyway. I try to pull something positive out of every situation. If I learn something, then it wasn't that bad after all; it taught me a lesson. Always keep in mind there could be a blessing on the other side of this lesson. That pain is attached to a promise. Seek God and find the purpose in the pain.

During stage III adolescent teens tend to become more independent. Some parents begin to experience nostalgia thinking of the times when their kids completely depended on them. Careful during this stage parents, it'll have you going and making babies that you did not originally plan for, ha! Adolescents are doing everything they can to separate and gain more freedom from their parents. The pupa on the other hand must be protected at all cost. Funny thing is, the adolescent and the pupa both need to be protected. Our parents have been where we are going, so naturally they want to shield us from unnecessary hurt. Not only do our parents try to protect us, so does God. Refer to Jeremiah 29:11 and trust Gods direction for your future.

He has a plan that's specifically designed and tailored for you, but you have to focus on Him and not what others are doing. Remember His plan is for you only. Think about when you find a pair of jeans that are the perfect fit. I know I get excited; they fit good through the hip, the length is right, no gap in the back, Yes! That's what God wants to do for your life. He won't leave any gaps. Guidance is important of course, but I think there are some things we just have to go through in order to grow. In order to fully understand what God is doing in our lives. Some seasons are strictly for Him to work His perfect plan through our lives, and the beautiful thing about God is that He causes it ALL to work for our good. Yes, even that. That thing you can't tell anybody. Not your momma, not your daddy, nobody. That thing that you've vowed to take to your grave. Yes, that too. Not some things, ALL things! (Romans 8:28)

Apply Pressure

Pressure: the burden of physical or mental distress
: the weight of social or economic imposition
: the stress of urgency of matters demanding attention

*O*kay, so a little pressure is often not a problem. In fact, it usually keeps us from being lazy. That assignment that you've had for weeks, is suddenly being completed because the due date is tomorrow. Summers over so the kids are finally getting to the dentist and doctor's appointments. See a little pressure is usually the extra push we need to go ahead and get things done. You get a small cut and want to stop bleeding, you're told to apply pressure. But what happens when the pressure becomes too great? Sadly, the pressures start as early as school age. Our kids are faced with the pressure to fit in. They want the latest shoes and clothes, and guess who that puts pressure on; the parents. Parents want their kids to have the best and there's no harm there. The problem comes when you're neglecting family time with them so that you can afford those expensive shoes and clothes. It's not just the kids though, adults do it as well. You feel pressured to go trade in your 2018 because your neighbor pulled up in a 2019. Just stop it. Be happy for people without feeling the need to one up them. You have to know that the same God that blessed them because it was their time will do the same for you when it's your time. Then there's pressure to be a good wife or husband. Pressure to keep the kids in good schools, pressure to be a good daughter, pressure to be a good friend. You're pressured to say yes when the answer should obviously be no. It's all unrealistic. Don't put this pressure on yourself, and don't allow others to place it on you. Refuse to be trapped by the enemy. Refuse to let comparisons rob you of your joy. The enemy loves using subtle ways to suck you into yet another daunting task that doesn't serve your purpose; yet we do it in an attempt to check off another step on our success ladder. We do it to appear to have it all together to everyone else when that couldn't be furthest from the truth.

Success looks very different for everyone. Some say they need a bank account full of money and an 800 credit score. Others may feel they need the nicest car on the lot. One says I've been on 6 different trips this year. Someone else is working tirelessly to pay off their mortgage and student loans. Another may look at their family, health and sound mind. I say it's all about balance. There is nothing wrong with having or doing things just be sure things don't have you. When we begin to mistreat our loved ones over material things we have lost sight of what is truly important. It would be no good for you to gain all these earthly things but lose your soul. (Mark 8:36)

Whatever success looks like to you choosing faith over fear will be beneficial in moving toward that success. I set out to achieve many goals, and I'm sure by now we've figured out that just because we set them, we aren't guaranteed to walk right into them. You will be met by opposition along the way. Something as simple as your daily routine of taking care of your family may get in the way. Set the goals anyway, and don't just set them; raise the bar. Activate that crazy faith. As my Pastor says, "get your hopes up!"

Before I had a good understanding of what it meant to persevere, that's what momma always told me to do. I'm sure some will relate, but I've always felt like I had to work a little harder to achieve my goals, but I don't mind as much now. It's all in how you look at it. I don't have a complaining spirit, and in everything I go through I'm constantly interested in learning. I'm so thankful that my family has always been so supportive. My parents and my brothers make me feel like I can achieve anything. I also have a small inner circle of friends and family who are supportive and hold me accountable.

I was told to persevere so often when things began to look uncertain I could hear it in my head. It taught me at an early age to keep pushing. Keep applying pressure. To keep pressing toward my goals regardless of how often I was met with difficulty. We must turn everything into a teachable situation. Who are you teaching? Or are you too busy marking those things off your list, you haven't stopped to help anyone else. Oh okay, no one helped you so you're not gonna help anybody, huh? Or maybe you're the one that feels like they didn't do it so they can't tell you anything; you would be surprised the things you can learn just by being quiet for a second. It cost you nothing to listen, offer a kind word, or a smile. Offer it today, it may be just what someone needs to keep going and apply pressure. You have to use a disclaimer when applying pressure though. Some people will wonder why you're still pursuing that goal you set 10 years ago. Persevere. Don't let up. Apply pressure. Soon they will begin to see that you're operating through a completely other realm.

> Not as though I had already attained, either were already perfect: but I follow after it that I may apprehend of Christ Jesus. Brethren, I count not myself to have apprehended: but this one thing I do, forgetting those things which are behind, and reaching forth into those things which are before I press toward the mark for the prize of the high calling of God in Christ Jesus. (Philippians 3:12-14)

~Prayer~

God, I know sometimes I get tired, but help me to not grow weary. God help me keep pressing forward for I know you are calling me higher. God give me the wisdom I need to accept the call and keep applying pressure. Help me oh God to not settle, but to keep seeking my purpose. In Jesus name, Amen.

Iron Sharpens Iron

$\mathcal{F}$riend, one attached to another by affection or esteem.

I take the word friend very seriously. I cherish my friendships, and the most important word in the definition is "attached." Our closest friends are usually who we spend most of our time with. Rather on the phone or in person. There is power in forming the right friendships. Our friends have the power of influence, and they will be able to speak into our lives. There are some instances where they won't even be aware that's what they are doing. What a blessing it will be if they are speaking edifying words. What a blessing if they are leading us closer to our purpose. As we grow older the seasons of our lives will change, and so will our friendships. Change is not always comfortable, but it is necessary. Hopefully you and your friends will grow together, even if it's at a different pace.

> "Iron sharpens iron; so a man sharpeneth the countenance of his friend." Proverbs 27:17

I'm a patient person I don't mind slow pace as long as we're progressing.

Quick side note. I think that's where we get ourselves in the most trouble, we get in a hurry. We have to learn to exercise more patience. We must learn to take beauty in stillness. I have personally found that I gain so much clarity when I take a few moments to be still. A few moments to silence all the noise around me. Sadly, a lot of us are so busy we won't be able to do that. Many are going nowhere fast. Just because you're busy does not mean you're fulfilling your purpose. Chasing more money, more things, but still have no inner peace. No closer to your dreams, and nothing to show for it except the bags under the eyes. Never satisfied.

> You have sown much, and bring in little; ye eat, but ye have not enough, ye drink, but ye are not filled with drink; ye clothe you, but there is none warm; and he that earneth wages earneth wages to put it into a bag with holes.

Haggai 1:6-7

What does that above verse have to do with you? You ever get done eating, and not feel full? Ever get paid on Thursday only to wonder where your check went on Friday? Are you being faithful to God with what you have? God provides your every need, and will do so without you running yourself ragged. God is saying, consider your ways. Take a second and do a self-check. Being tired all the time, stressed out, stretched too thin, and not honoring Him; that's not kingdom. What if we had the kind of friends that would ask questions to make sure we're in tune with what we should be doing. Not just, "hey you wanna go grab some drinks" or hey you wanna go on this trip" or "hey you wanna go to the club." It's nothing wrong with having a good time within reason, but when we are in fruitful friendships they tell us what we need to hear even when it isn't easy for us to hear it. If you don't have those kinds of friends, you many need to re-evaluate your circle. Furthermore, if you're not being that friend; start today. You aren't doing your friends any favors by agreeing with their wrongs. Tell people the truth in love.

Just like the pruning we have to do with plants, we have to do that in our lives. I remember receiving some plants and I was so excited. After getting them planted, one was thriving beautifully, but the other one was barely coming along. I'm no gardener so I struggled with rather it was okay to cut it. After reading about the plant we knew it had to be cut. It wasn't long before the plant began to grow as beautiful as the other one. I encourage you to do the same in your life. Cut off those toxic, life sucking, energy draining, growth stunting relationships. You can love them; you can pray for them; just do so from afar. Often we don't realize the weight of something until we put it down. Rid yourself of that extra weight. The bible says to everything there is a season. (Ecclesiastes 3:1-8)

Some of the people we meet will be with us forever. Just as there are some people of whom we will love forever. If you're a lover of people and a giver sometimes you allow people to stay when the season has clearly changed. Don't. I understand how hard it can be, but you have to allow some friendships and relationships to dissolve. It doesn't have to be complicated or confrontational, but it has to end. You don't even have to worry yourself with conjuring up this wordy script as to why it's over. Just know that it simply has to be. There are some places God's taking you and everyone can't go. Also, don't let the amount of time you've known someone keep them around for a season they shouldn't be in. I enjoy leftovers as much as the next person, but quit rewarming food that needs to be thrown out. Quit giving life to dead situations. DNR. (Do Not Resuscitate).

~Prayer~

God, I thank you for my fruitful friendships. I'm grateful for the love and loyalty that we share for I know it is truly a rare gift. Lord I'm so glad that iron sharpens iron. Lord I thank you for friends that can show me the way, and remind me of who and whose I am when I seem to have lost my way. God keep me mindful that in order to have these kinds of friends I must first show myself friendly. In Jesus name, Amen.

Stage IV

"For I know the plans I have for you, "declares the Lord," plans to prosper you and not to harm you, plans to give you a hope and a future. (Jeremiah 29:11)

Human~Adult   Butterfly~Adult

Your Wings Are Ready!

ot chicken wings, ha! Most of the time when people talk about wings, they're either going to pick up some garlic parmesan flats or they're referring to someone who has passed away. He or she gained their wings. Contrary to popular belief living our best life is not reserved for when we get to heaven. God taught us in which manner to pray, and it says, "in earth", "as it is in heaven". When we begin to operate under the authority that has been given to us by Jesus Christ we gain a much better understanding of that. We realize that when we completely surrender ourselves to God and his will for our lives we won't be lacking anything.

In stage IV humans and butterflies alike are considered adults. For us humans, we're like Yes! This is it! 18 and can finally have that freedom from my parents. The truth is even with the best parents there is no way for them to teach us everything. Just as the butterfly is rested and is now ready to fly there are still things that need to take place before they take flight. The butterflies have to get their blood flowing and wings to flapping before they actually learn to fly. Guess what, they aren't even good fliers in the beginning. The key is proper guidance and wise counsel freely given in love. Don't despise that person closest to you with the very strong opinion who attempts to speak into your life.

Though I used to prepare meals for my younger brother and I; it wasn't until my 2nd year of college that I learned to properly fry an egg. Yes, you read it right. I dropped the egg in the pan with no oil, scratched up my roommate, Kenyettas nice pan and took the egg sandwich in there with no butter, no salt and pepper; nothing, lol. That's right, something as simple as fixing an egg sandwich can slide through the cracks. I turned out okay though, and these days I make a mean egg sandwich and I enjoy cooking. You see there are some things we will learn along the way. Or as I've discovered; unlearn. Part of being an adult is accepting that you have to unlearn and relearn in order to keep growing.

Stage IV or the Adult stage is where we take all the skills, and go out and conquer the world. The truth is we quickly realize that there is so much more for us to absorb. The best thing we can do for ourselves is to always be open and remain teachable. Never get to a point where no one can tell you anything. Remain open and go get your wings. Emerge from your chrysalis season and go be all God has created you to be. Side bar: those very parents you were so eager to get free from at 18 are the very ones who will bring you the most comfort at 30.

From Worry to Worship

Worship: to honor or reverence as a divine being or supernatural power.

Worry: to torment oneself with or suffer from disturbing thoughts; fret

We won't be giving life to dead situations, but we will be getting our entire life through worship. That means you'll learn how worship has the power to bring so much peace to your life. If we're not worshipping we're probably worrying. When we worship it shifts our focus from worry, and helps us center our minds on the one who can take those worries away, and His name is Jesus. It's okay if you don't have all the answers. It is also okay, to not be okay; just don't stay there. I've been in church my whole life, and I was once quite the worrier. You do know that simply attending church won't automatically fix things. You have to be a willing participant. You have to allow the word to penetrate your heart. We don't just go to church; we are the church. It wasn't until someone said to me "you go to church every Sunday, you pray and believe, why do you worry so much?" It's like I had an epiphany in that moment. There I was inviting them to church, but not living like I believed what God said. I made a decision at that moment to change that and not be that person ever again. For some people during their season in our lives we will be the only church they see. Ask yourself what am I displaying to them? How am I representing Christ? It's easy to worship God when everything around you is going good. Your family is healthy, your money is flowing, you got the promotion at work, your marriage is thriving, but are you willing to worship Him when you're counting change to make the rent. I'll count the change, and thank Him in advance for my better days; because they are coming. Will you praise Him when you've done all you know to do with your rebellious teen? Will you still praise Him when your heart is aching from the turmoil in your marriage? Will you praise Him when the car is acting up; yet again. Will you praise Him after the rape? What about when your relationship is awkward with your mom?

There's so much power in worship. There's freedom in worship, deliverance in worship, healing in worship. When you choose to worship and praise God in spite of it confuses the enemy. It's such an amazing experience when you usher in the presence of God all by yourself. Not because its Sunday, and it's time for worship but because you need it right where you are. I enjoy all kinds of music, but when I put on my favorite worship songs my mood changes instantly. There is just something about the name of Jesus! There is a shift in the atmosphere.

Although I love to sing alone; lol. You don't have to be able to carry a tune just allow the music to minister to you. I've had people tell me they can't join my church because they can't get with the music. I mean that's your prerogative, but I wouldn't dare miss out on the truth of God's word being taught because I couldn't get with the music. No judgement here though I understood that to worship God on a deeper level you have to have experienced the glory of Him at a certain level. Until you've encountered an experience where you saw God move, and you know without one doubt that it was only Him that moved, then and only then will you give him all the praise. You have to listen to the words. True worship is not just about a sound that makes you feel good and run up and down the aisles. It's a heart thing. It's where we get to honor God simply because of who He is. Simply because He is worthy! God is so many things. He's a healer. He's a provider, a father to the fatherless but above all He is worthy. When we come to truly know God and understand who He is it takes our worship to a completely different level. I'm not talking about religion; but relationship. Worship gives us a chance to take our minds off the world and center it on God. Bow before the King, fall on your knees, adore Him, worship Him in spirit and in truth. Why? Because He is worthy!

~Prayer~

God I trust you; completely. In my trusting you, help me to be a warrior and not a worrier. God I know when I surrender myself to you a shift happens. Lord I thank you for the truth of your word. Thank you for revealing yourself to me. Lord I worship you forever and I give you all the praise. In Jesus name, Amen.

I Choose Life…
I Choose to be Grateful

Gratitude: the state of being grateful; thankfulness

There are so many wonderful things I love about God, but at the top of the list has to be that fact that He gives us free will. Free will to choose.

To choose means that we can freely decide one way over the other. Isn't that great? He doesn't force us to do anything. (Deuteronomy 30:19-20)

With the exceptions of a few scrooges usually most people tend to be in a better mood around the holidays. I often say I wonder how much different our lives would be if people were in the "holiday spirit" all year long. Everyone joins in on the singing. People smile more. Some people even look up from their phones long enough to actually say good morning, Happy Thanksgiving or Merry Christmas. There is just something about the holidays that bring everyone together. Rather it's reaching out to that friend who's lost someone or getting together with your cousins, aunts and uncles. We just seem to think about, and consider everyone around these times. "It's the thought that counts" I am sure we have heard it or even said it ourselves. Well, what if we gave that much attention to the thoughts we think every day; because it really is the thought that counts. When we get our thoughts right it sets the tone for the course of our lives. Philippians 4:8, says whatever is pure and true are the things we should be thinking about. I would really like to see us living our lives this way on the daily. Living with a grateful heart. Thankful that we're able to see a new day. Thankful that God's mercies are new every morning. Thankful that if we got it wrong yesterday, today we can make it right. I love that one. I've been known to give way too many chances, but I live my life by the standard of extending the same grace that I so freely receive from God. Thank you Jesus for your grace and mercy!

We have to learn to not be so easily moved by our emotions, and appreciate the sun as well as the rain. No one wants to have rain all the time, but its during that rain that we usually sit still long enough to appreciate when the sun shines. Lord, I thank You for the rain. Too often we take it for granted.

Be intentional about not letting the circumstances change the condition of your heart. I was taught at a young age no matter how small the gesture to always be thankful and to express gratitude. It holds true to this day, it's so important for me to let people know how much I appreciate things they do for me, and how much they mean to me. Momma always says, "give me my flowers while I'm still here, because I can't smell them when I'm gone." Sometimes we focus so much on the future, that we often miss golden opportunities to spread love in the moment. Many of us can't appreciate a great thing, because we are too busy looking for the next thing. Rather that great thing is an unforgettable moment with family or an unforgettable person who crossed your path; cherish it. Life is not a destination, it's a journey that we're forever learning and we should enjoy it. We should always choose joy, and choose to praise God in spite of. All hell may be breaking loose around us and there may be a full on war taking place, but praise Him anyway.

Love your neighbor anyway. Honor your parents anyway. Praise your way through. God is faithful! When you make a choice to be grateful and have joy it does not mean you will be exempt from problems. (Matthew 5:44-45)

It's all about your mindset. You may have these problems, but they don't have you! I'll tell my secret since I want us all to be free. I have found the secret to true happiness is having a grateful heart. Where do you start? I'm glad you asked. We've been operating with child-like faith right? Use your child- like faith paired with your adult wisdom to realize that the blood still works. Start declaring the blood of Jesus over every area of your life that's keeping you from having a grateful heart. Release anger, bitterness, jealousy, resentment, strife. Free yourself and loose it all. Take the lessons from every stage of your life and let that be the tenacity you need to choose life; to choose to be grateful in spite of and keep pressing forward. (I Thessalonians 5:18)

~Prayer~

Dear God, thank you.

I thank you for who you are and what you've been in my life. I thank you for waking me up this morning and allowing me to see a new day. I thank you for your grace and mercy. I'm so thankful that your mercies are new every morning, and I don't have to live today off of yesterday's mercy. Thank you for chasing me down. Thank you for fighting for me. In this moment I just wanna thank you for everything you've done. Thank you for my family. Thank you for the gift of true friendship. Thank you for shielding me from seen and unforeseen dangers. Lord, thank you for keeping me. Thank you for covering me, and keeping me in my right mind. Thank you for delivering me from evil! I'm so grateful. Thank you for giving me the strength to endure when I began to grow weary. Thank you for patience. Thank you for wisdom to know how to wait. Thank you for another opportunity to get it right and pursue my God given purpose. In Jesus name, Amen.

Nuggets of Wisdom

Introduction

Use your child-like faith to gain a new perspective on the seasons of your life.

Allow yourself to be completely transformed by the renewing of your mind.

Waiting Patiently

Trust God completely. He only needs a willing vessel. Give Him all the glory.

When you receive a report, take it to the highest court. Man says, but what does God say.

Chapter 1

Tell everyone about something that helped you. Be the person you needed growing up.

When frustration, doubt, or disappointments creep in cast those thoughts down. What does the word of God say?

Chapter 2

Tap into your God given gift and activate the power on the inside of you.

Completely surrender and be transformed for the glory of God.

Don't be held captive by false thoughts.

All You Can Eat

There will be tests but turn them into testimonies. You will not be defeated.

Don't just go through; Grow through!

Chapter 3

Thank you God for the gift of hindsight. I will use my 20/20 vision to make better choices.

God I trust you, and I will forever follow after you.

Chapter 4

Choose Faith over fear daily.

Take the limits off God. Stop making Him so small.

Have radical faith and take God at His word.

#1 Constant is Change

Some of your most uncomfortable situations will yield the most amazing change in your life. Allow it.

Be a Warrior not a worrier.

Chapter 5

There is nothing wrong with having things just don't let things have you

Persevere

Don't have a complaining spirit

Chapter 6

Iron sharpens Iron

Our friends have power of influence

DNR. Do NOT resuscitate. Quit giving life to dead situations.

Your Wings Are Ready

Accept wise counsel freely given in love.

It's okay to learn some things along the way.

Chapter 7

True worship is a heart thing

Honor God simply because He is worthy.

Bow before the King. Worship Him in spirit and in truth.

Chapter 8

Choose Joy. Praise God in spite of...

God is Faithful!

Give people their flowers while they are still here; they can't smell them once they're gone

The blood still works!

Fly boldly into your God given purpose!

Do Your Work

Take a few minutes from your daily routine to "do your work". These are just a few simple questions, but I believe the answers can hold so much weight. Many of the disappointments in our lives are brought on by unfulfilled expectations that we place on ourselves. No one is here, and no one has to see your answers. Be truthful with yourself so that you can begin to be set free.

1. What dreams did you have as a child that you've given up on because you feel they are out of your reach?

2. How has your life been affected by not fulfilling those dreams?

3a. What will it take to make those dreams come true? 3b. How passionate are you about making what it takes happen?

4. How has your relationship with God been altered as a result of not seeing these changes in your life?

5. What past hurt do you need to release in order to soar high into your God given purpose?

You've Got Your Wings

In Closing

This whole adventure started because I was crazy enough to activate my child-like faith and tap into my lifelong love of butterflies and writing. Though life will give you much uncertainty trust that God has went on before you and perfected your path. Bend, but don't break. What happens when we realize there's strength in our wings? We're completely transformed; forever. Ask God to search you. Ask Him to come into your heart and remove everything that's not like Him. Release your pride, fear, and shame. Let those tests be a testimony that you didn't just go through, but you GREW through. Allow your testimony to become the momentum you need to propel you into your God given purpose.

I was having a phone conversation with my dad one day and I wasn't complaining just running down the things that I had been doing in general conversation sharing like we always do now that I am an adult. Most of the time I talk to the Lord, especially if it's a big decision I need to make, but there were some things on my heart, and in that moment it's like God spoke through my dad. My dad was his usual calm corky self, but the message was simple; yet loud and clear. "Well daughter, bend, but don't break." So as you read I say to you, **BEND, BUT DON'T BREAK**. As long as there is oxygen in your body there is time to fulfill your purpose. Truthfully if you live the right way your purpose will continue to be fulfilled long after you're gone. We're all struggling to overcome something. Choices you made or someone just flat out bringing bad energy. God has the power to do a mighty work and transform you beyond anything you could ever do on your own. I pray you will allow it. Make a decision today to be restored. So, what happens when we realize there's strength in our wings? We're changed forever.

Are you ready to soar? Are you ready to reach heights you never dreamed of? We all have a different story. Though similar each of our paths are unique. We also all have an enemy whose #1 goal is to keep us from flying high and reaching our God given purpose. Life will meet us with all kinds of opposition, but just how bad do you want it? How passionate are you about being in line with the will of God for your life?

My prayer is that you will allow the Holy Spirit to remind you to keep pressing forward. If God has called you, then he's also equipped you. Get up; get dressed. Look the part, give it all you've got and trust God to do the rest. God can do amazing things for you if you just let Him. He may switch the play or run a different route but surrender it all to Him and go make the biggest most celebrated play of your life. The road ahead may begin to get bumpy and rough, but feel the turbulence, and keep flying high; you're on your way to new heights. Uncharted territory. Trust God completely and get ready to experience your life in extraordinary ways.

All my love,

Jessica Lynette

CPSIA information can be obtained
at www.ICGtesting.com
Printed in the USA
LVHW081101051119
PP15346100001B/9/P